How Hackers Work (and How to Stop Them)

Common Scams, Phishing, Malware, and Real-World Tactics Used by Cybercriminals

By Joe Correa

Published by Live Stronger Faster

This book is for educational and informational purposes only. The author and publisher are not engaged in rendering legal, financial, or other professional advice. Readers should consult a qualified professional before making any financial decisions.

First Edition

Table of Contents

Introduction

In today's digital world, cybercrime has become one of the most profitable and dangerous industries on the planet. Every year, individuals and businesses lose billions of dollars to hackers—many of whom use simple but effective tactics that most people never see coming. Whether it's a phishing email that looks like it's from your bank or a fake pop-up asking you to "update" your software, cybercriminals are always adapting—and they're getting more convincing every day.

This book was created to help you fight back. You don't need to be a tech expert to defend yourself. You just need to understand how hackers think, what tactics they use, and how to build simple habits that make you a hard target.

In **Book 3**, we'll uncover the secrets of how hackers operate, from traditional scams to modern-day ransomware attacks. You'll learn the difference between phishing and spear phishing, what malware really does, how social engineering tricks you into giving away sensitive data, and how hackers target both individuals and businesses with tailored attacks.

This book is packed with real-world examples of attacks—some clever, some terrifying—and practical steps you can take right now to protect yourself and your family. You'll also learn how to identify red flags, recognize scam attempts, and respond quickly if your system is compromised.

We'll break everything down in simple, clear language so that even complete beginners can understand how to recognize threats and stop hackers in their tracks.

Let's pull back the curtain and reveal what's really going on behind the scenes of cybercrime—so you can stay safe, alert, and in control.

Chapter 1: Inside the Hacker's Mind

To defend yourself against cybercrime, you must first understand your adversary. Hackers are not just mysterious figures in hoodies typing rapidly in dark rooms. They are real people with diverse goals, backgrounds, and tools. Some work for governments, some are part of global criminal networks, and others are simply curious or driven by ego. But what unites them all is a deep understanding of how digital systems—and human behavior—can be exploited.

Let's begin by classifying hackers. There are three primary types: **black hat**, **white hat**, and **gray hat**. Black hat hackers are the bad actors—criminals who break into systems to steal, damage, or ransom information for personal gain. They operate outside the law and are responsible for most of the cyberattacks reported in the news. White hat hackers, on the other hand, are ethical hackers who use their skills to help organizations strengthen their cybersecurity. They often work as penetration testers or security consultants. Gray hat hackers live in the murky middle. They may break into systems without permission but don't always have malicious intent. Sometimes, they expose vulnerabilities publicly in the hopes of pressuring companies to improve security.

Understanding **motivation** is another critical step. Not all hackers are motivated by money. Some hack for political reasons—these are called **hacktivists**. Others want to prove their skills to gain respect in the hacker community or for personal revenge. Still others are state-sponsored actors who engage in cyber espionage to steal secrets or disrupt foreign governments. Then, there are opportunists—people who stumble upon weak systems and simply can't resist exploiting them.

Hackers follow a structured process when launching an attack. This is known as the **hacker lifecycle**, and it usually includes the following steps:

1. **Reconnaissance**: Hackers gather information about the target. This can include scanning a company's website, LinkedIn profiles, or even social media posts for vulnerabilities or employee details.

2. **Scanning and Enumeration**: They use automated tools to identify open ports, exposed databases, or outdated software.

3. **Exploitation**: This is when the hacker breaks into the system—usually by exploiting a known vulnerability or tricking a user into giving up credentials.

4. **Privilege Escalation**: Once inside, the hacker works

to gain higher levels of access—such as admin rights.

5. **Maintaining Access**: Backdoors or malware may be installed so the hacker can return later, even if passwords are changed.

6. **Covering Tracks**: Logs are erased or altered to avoid detection.

7. **Exfiltration or Damage**: This is the final goal—stealing sensitive data, installing ransomware, or causing operational disruption.

While this lifecycle is typical of black hat hackers, understanding it helps everyone—from individuals to small businesses—recognize where and how to block attacks.

Contrary to popular belief, most successful cyberattacks don't rely on high-level technical wizardry. Instead, they rely on exploiting **human vulnerabilities**. Hackers know people are the weakest link in any system. That's why tactics like phishing emails, fake tech support calls, and impersonation are so effective. Even a highly secure server becomes vulnerable if someone clicks on a malicious link or reuses a password that's already been leaked.

There's also a myth that only large corporations are targets. In reality, small businesses and individuals are prime targets because they often have weaker defenses. A freelancer's Gmail account, a retiree's online banking app, or a teenager's gaming login could all be entry points to more valuable data or larger networks.

Hackers use **open-source intelligence (OSINT)** to research their victims. With just a name and email address, they can dig into public records, social media, and data breach archives to build detailed profiles. This helps them craft convincing phishing emails, guess passwords, or answer security questions. The more data you leave exposed, the easier you are to hack.

As cybercriminals grow more organized, some have begun offering **"hacking as a service."** This means even someone without technical skills can pay for access to tools like ransomware kits, phishing templates, or stolen credentials on the dark web. This democratization of cybercrime means the number of attacks is skyrocketing—and the barriers to entry are shrinking.

But there's good news: most attacks are preventable. By understanding how hackers think and operate, you can shift from being an easy target to a hardened one. It starts with awareness—knowing how attacks are launched, what motivates them, and how you can disrupt that process.

In the coming chapters, we'll dissect specific attack types and show you how to protect yourself against them. But always remember: cybercriminals thrive on ignorance and complacency. The more informed you are, the less power they have over your digital life.

Jake's story

Jake Morgan sat in the corner of a dimly lit café in Austin, Texas, sipping an espresso and tapping away on his laptop. He looked just like any other digital nomad—hoodie, noise-canceling headphones, focused expression. But Jake wasn't writing a blog post or editing a startup pitch deck. He was scanning a hotel's employee login portal on the other side of the country.

His target was a mid-sized hotel chain with outdated security practices—exactly the kind of company Jake specialized in exploiting. He wasn't trying to hurt anyone, or so he told himself. This was his job. He was a gray hat hacker, walking the tightrope between legal and illegal. And today, he was about to cross that line again.

Earlier that morning, Jake had started his routine with **reconnaissance**. A quick glance at the hotel's LinkedIn page revealed a few dozen employees, including an operations manager who loved posting about work on social media. In one photo, Jake spotted a monitor in the background displaying a staff dashboard. Zooming in, he caught a glimpse of the portal URL—gold. He now knew where to aim.

Using open-source tools, Jake scanned the login page for vulnerabilities. He discovered it was using outdated software, unpatched for months. With a few keystrokes, he initiated a script that tested for known exploits. Ten minutes later, he was in—not fully, but he had access to the outer walls of the system.

His heart beat a little faster. **Exploitation** was next. He tried a default password: admin123. It failed. He tried password1. Still nothing. Then he guessed the operations manager's email and added the birth year he found on her Facebook profile. Bingo.

Once inside, Jake began **escalating privileges**. He searched the internal directories and found a hidden admin panel. No two-factor authentication. No alerts. Like a guest who had stolen a master key, he was now free to roam every room in the building—digitally speaking.

He didn't steal any credit card numbers. Instead, he copied data logs, backend files, and internal documents into a compressed folder and encrypted it. He left a note in the logs: "You've been breached. Patch your system. Here's how. No ransom. Just a warning." It was a classic gray hat move—an unsanctioned penetration test. Some companies welcomed the warning. Others called the FBI.

As Jake packed up and left the café, he felt both a thrill and a pang of guilt. He had technically broken the law, but he justified it in his head as a necessary wake-up call for a company that had left its digital doors wide open.

Three states away, Olivia Castillo was having a very different morning. She worked in finance for the same hotel chain Jake had just breached. As she sipped her coffee, her email pinged. "Urgent: Please confirm payroll details by 10 a.m." The message came from what appeared to be the CFO's address, using company language and formatting. She clicked the link without thinking and logged into the system.

Moments later, her credentials were in the hands of a very different kind of hacker—a **black hat** operating out of Eastern Europe. Unlike Jake, this hacker didn't care about warning messages or ethical lines. Within minutes, he began siphoning off employee data, including Social Security numbers and direct deposit info. He installed a backdoor and erased the login history to cover his tracks. Then he sold the data on a dark web forum for $2,500.

By the time IT noticed the breach three days later, it was too late. Dozens of employees had already reported fraudulent activity. The hotel's reputation was crumbling, and Olivia was sick with anxiety, blaming herself for clicking the link.

Across the digital landscape, another hacker was just getting started. Lily, a teenage **white hat hacker**, was participating in a government-sponsored cybersecurity competition. Her task: break into a mock company's system, find the weaknesses, and report them. She did exactly that—finding a misconfigured firewall that exposed sensitive APIs. Instead of exploiting it, she submitted her report and earned a $5,000 bug bounty.

Three hackers. Three motivations. One battlefield.

Jake hacked for the challenge and moral high ground. The Eastern European attacker hacked for money and chaos. Lily hacked to learn and protect. Yet all three used similar methods—scanning, exploiting, escalating, and evading detection. What made the difference wasn't their skills. It was their ethics.

The story of hacking is not just one of code and computers. It's about psychology, persuasion, and power. Some hackers manipulate machines. The most dangerous ones manipulate people. They study behaviors, exploit emotions, and weaponize trust.

And as long as people continue to click suspicious links, reuse passwords, and trust unfamiliar emails, hackers will continue to win.

But stories like these don't have to end in disaster. Understanding how hackers think—their tactics, their tools, and their weaknesses—is the first step in fighting back. Because the best way to stay safe in the digital age is to stop thinking like a victim… and start thinking like a hacker.

Chapter 2: The Anatomy of a Phishing Attack

Phishing is one of the most common and successful hacking techniques used today—not because it's highly technical, but because it preys on human behavior. A phishing attack tricks people into giving away confidential information by impersonating a trusted source. It's the digital version of a con artist showing up at your front door, pretending to be the cable guy, and walking out with your wallet.

The anatomy of a phishing attack begins with **deception**. The attacker creates a message, usually an email or text, that appears to come from a credible source—your bank, employer, a government agency, or even a friend. These messages are designed to create a sense of **urgency**, **fear**, or **curiosity** to pressure the recipient into acting quickly without thinking critically.

A basic phishing email might say something like, *"Your account has been compromised. Click here to reset your password."* But more advanced versions, known as **spear phishing**, are tailored specifically to the target. They may include the recipient's name, job title, or references to recent activity—often gathered from social media or public databases.

The more personalized the email, the more convincing it becomes.

Let's break down the typical components of a phishing email:

1. **The Sender Address**: Often mimics a real domain but includes subtle misspellings, such as "apple-support.com" instead of "apple.com." Some attackers even spoof the email header to make it appear identical to a legitimate sender.

2. **The Subject Line**: Designed to get immediate attention. Examples include:

    - *"Urgent: Account Suspension Notice"*
    - *"Invoice Overdue – Action Required"*
    - *"You've Been Selected for a Tax Refund"*

3. **The Body of the Email**: Uses fear or opportunity to pressure the recipient. It may ask the user to verify an account, claim a prize, or view a document. The tone often mimics professional language.

4. **The Link or Attachment**: This is the real payload. Clicking the link may lead to a fake website designed to

steal credentials. Opening an attachment could install malware or ransomware.

5. **The Fake Website**: These sites look identical to the real thing but are hosted on fraudulent domains. Users who aren't paying close attention might enter usernames, passwords, or credit card numbers that go directly to the attacker.

Once a victim clicks the link and submits information, the hacker typically uses it in real time. If login credentials are stolen, they may be tested immediately on multiple services. If banking details are captured, money may be transferred within minutes.

There are also **variants** of phishing beyond email.

- **Smishing** is phishing via SMS or messaging apps.
- **Vishing** is voice phishing—fraudulent phone calls pretending to be tech support or customer service.
- **Clone phishing** replicates legitimate past emails and adds a malicious attachment.
- **Business Email Compromise (BEC)** attacks trick employees into wiring money or sharing sensitive information by impersonating a CEO or executive.

So why do people still fall for phishing? The answer is simple: these attacks target emotions, not logic. The best phishing emails are designed to bypass your brain's reasoning process by creating panic, greed, or trust.

One of the biggest vulnerabilities is the **lack of verification habits**. Most users do not double-check URLs, sender email addresses, or message formatting. They assume legitimacy based on brand logos, professional language, or the urgency of the request.

Even highly trained professionals fall for phishing attacks—especially during high-stress times like tax season, election periods, or when major events dominate the news. Hackers often time their attacks during public crises when people are distracted or overwhelmed.

To defend yourself, here are some core **anti-phishing strategies**:

- **Hover Before You Click**: On a computer, always hover over links to reveal the actual URL before clicking.
- **Verify the Sender**: Look for small differences in the sender's email address. Be cautious of public email

providers like Gmail or Yahoo being used by supposed institutions.

- **Check Grammar and Formatting**: Many phishing messages contain awkward grammar, strange phrases, or inconsistent branding.
- **Don't Click Unfamiliar Links or Open Unexpected Attachments**: Even if the message appears to be from a trusted source, verify through a separate communication channel before opening anything.
- **Use Multi-Factor Authentication (MFA)**: This way, even if your password is compromised, your account remains protected by a second verification step.
- **Report Suspicious Emails**: Most platforms and companies have ways to report phishing attempts. Doing so helps protect others.
- **Train Yourself and Your Team**: Phishing awareness training—especially in small businesses—can dramatically reduce the risk of falling for these attacks.

Also, consider using browser extensions and email filters that scan for phishing attempts automatically. Tools like **Google Safe Browsing**, **Microsoft Defender SmartScreen**, and

PhishTank can warn users about suspicious websites and links.

Ultimately, the success of phishing depends on a moment of distraction. The attacker is betting that you're too busy, stressed, or tired to scrutinize an email that looks real enough. But once you train yourself to pause, verify, and think critically about every digital communication—phishing loses its power.

The best protection is not software—it's skepticism. Question everything. Trust cautiously. And never let urgency rush you into a mistake.

Now, let's go over Derrick's story

Derrick Chen had just finished his second cup of coffee when the email hit his inbox. The subject line read: **URGENT: Payroll Access Suspended – Please Update Credentials**

It was from "HR@empiretechpayroll.com," and it looked legit. Derrick worked as a regional manager at EmpireTech, a fast-growing software firm, and HR notices like this weren't unusual—especially during quarterly audits. He glanced at the clock. 9:17 AM. His day was already packed, and he didn't want to risk payroll issues for his team.

He clicked the link.

The page that opened looked identical to EmpireTech's payroll portal—same logo, same color scheme, same login box. Without thinking twice, Derrick typed in his username and password and hit "Login." The page flickered, then redirected him to a generic error page. He sighed, assumed it was a glitch, and moved on with his day.

Two hours later, the real damage began.

Across the world, in a cramped apartment in Manila, a cybercriminal named Rico leaned back in his chair and smiled. The credentials had worked. Derrick's access granted him entry not just to payroll records, but to tax forms, bank routing numbers, and employee SSNs. Rico didn't even need to do much digging. The portal had everything nicely organized. He packaged the data, encrypted it, and uploaded it to a darknet marketplace, where stolen credentials and personal records sold like gold.

By noon, Rico had earned $1,200 from the breach. Derrick, still oblivious, was handling a client call when the company's security team flagged unauthorized access from the Philippines. Within minutes, the account was locked—but the damage was already done.

When EmpireTech's IT department reached out to Derrick, he was stunned. "I thought it was from HR," he stammered. "The logo was the same. The wording sounded right." But it wasn't. A closer look at the email revealed subtle clues—like the sender's domain "empiretechpayroll.com" instead of the real "empiretech.com." The email body also had slight grammatical inconsistencies and oddly urgent language.

Derrick wasn't stupid. He was just busy. Distracted. Moving fast. And that's exactly what Rico counted on.

Phishing didn't rely on genius hacking. It relied on **psychology**.

Meanwhile, across the city, Alicia Monroe was checking her phone during her lunch break when she got a text message: **CHASE ALERT: Suspicious login detected. Click here to secure your account.**

The link looked official. The message used real Chase branding. But Alicia hesitated. She remembered a phishing awareness workshop from months ago where the speaker said, "Don't trust links in messages. Go directly to the source."

She closed the message, opened the official Chase app, and logged in. No alerts. No issues. Her account was fine.

Relieved, Alicia forwarded the message to Chase's fraud team and deleted it.

Alicia had almost been **smished**—a phishing attempt via SMS. Her decision to double-check saved her time, money, and stress. But many people weren't as cautious.

Back in Rico's world, phishing was a numbers game. He didn't need every email to work. He just needed one in a hundred. So, he used kits—automated templates with fake login pages, professional formatting, and even fake CAPTCHA tests to build trust. The kits were updated regularly to match the most popular platforms: Microsoft 365, PayPal, Google, Facebook, and corporate payroll systems.

Rico used public data to improve his hit rate. He scanned LinkedIn profiles for job titles, anniversaries, and recent promotions. He scraped email addresses from breached databases. He tailored messages to fit current events—offering fake vaccine updates during the pandemic, tax refund links during IRS season, and delivery alerts during holidays.

He even ran **BEC attacks**—Business Email Compromise—by impersonating executives and asking employees to buy gift cards or send wire transfers. In one case, he tricked an assistant into sending $7,500 to a fake vendor account, just by mimicking her boss's tone and signature.

But not all phishing stories ended in losses.

At a mid-sized accounting firm in Chicago, an employee named Lila received an email from what looked like her CEO, asking for confidential client data. She paused. Something felt off. The email didn't use the CEO's typical phrasing, and there was an odd spacing issue in the signature.

Instead of replying, Lila picked up the phone and called her boss directly.

"Did you just email me about tax files?" she asked.

"No. What email?"

She forwarded it to IT. Within minutes, they discovered the company was being targeted in a spear phishing campaign, likely tied to a recent breach at a third-party provider. Thanks to Lila's hesitation, the firm dodged a major data leak.

These stories reveal the full anatomy of phishing: it's not about hacking code—it's about **hacking trust**. Attackers know you're busy. They know you won't scrutinize every email. They prey on your stress, your schedule, and your assumptions.

But when you slow down, verify, and think before you click—you break their game.

Derrick's mistake was a reminder of how real the risk is. Alicia and Lila's caution showed how even small acts of skepticism can save entire companies.

In the next chapter, we'll go deeper into how hackers manipulate human behavior—how they exploit emotion, authority, and urgency to gain access to your digital world.

Because phishing is just the beginning.

Chapter 3: Social Engineering – How Hackers Trick You

Social engineering is the art of manipulating people into revealing confidential information or performing actions that compromise security. It's not about hacking systems—it's about hacking humans. While technical vulnerabilities can be patched with software updates, human vulnerabilities are far harder to fix. That's why social engineering is one of the most dangerous and successful tools in a hacker's arsenal.

At its core, social engineering relies on exploiting psychological triggers like trust, fear, urgency, authority, curiosity, and the desire to help. Instead of brute-forcing passwords or cracking encryption, social engineers study behavior, emotions, and social dynamics. They impersonate, manipulate, and deceive their way past digital defenses—often without writing a single line of malicious code.

There are several common **types of social engineering attacks**, each designed to target specific emotional or psychological weaknesses:

1. **Pretexting**: This involves creating a fabricated scenario (or pretext) to convince a victim to share information or grant access. For example, a hacker may

pose as an IT technician and claim they need remote access to fix a technical issue.

2. **Baiting**: Similar to phishing, baiting involves offering something enticing—like a free download, gift card, or USB drive—in exchange for access. Plugging in an infected USB labeled "Employee Bonus List" is a classic baiting tactic.

3. **Tailgating (or Piggybacking)**: This physical form of social engineering occurs when an attacker follows an authorized employee into a secure building or room by pretending to have forgotten their badge.

4. **Quid Pro Quo**: The attacker offers something in return for information. This might be posing as a survey taker offering a prize in exchange for login credentials, or fake tech support offering "help" in exchange for access.

5. **Impersonation and Authority**: Attackers pretend to be someone in power—like a CEO, bank manager, or government official. Victims are often afraid to question someone they perceive as an authority figure, especially when urgency is used.

6. **Reverse Social Engineering**: This technique manipulates the victim into initiating contact. For example, a hacker creates a fake issue (like crashing a system) and then poses as the solution-provider, waiting for someone to ask for help.

Social engineering attacks can happen **online**, **over the phone**, or **in person**. What makes them particularly dangerous is that they don't require any technical vulnerability—just human trust and a convincing story.

Let's walk through how a social engineering attack typically unfolds:

- **Reconnaissance**: The attacker researches the target. This may involve reviewing social media posts, LinkedIn profiles, or company websites to gather personal details, employee hierarchies, and behavioral cues.

- **Planning the Approach**: Based on their research, the attacker decides what kind of pretext or persona to use. The message, tone, and context are all tailored to the target.

- **Initiating Contact**: The hacker reaches out via phone, email, message, or in person. They often build rapport quickly, using familiarity, confidence, or flattery to lower defenses.

- **Exploitation**: The attacker asks for specific actions—click a link, provide login credentials, allow remote access, or forward sensitive information.
- **Exit Strategy**: A successful social engineer leaves no trace. They may end the conversation casually, thank the victim, or even compliment them for being "so helpful."

One of the reasons social engineering is so effective is **cognitive bias**. We're hardwired to trust people who seem confident, helpful, or like us. In the digital world, this bias is amplified by the lack of face-to-face cues and the tendency to respond quickly to messages.

Social engineers also exploit **emotional pressure**. A classic tactic is combining authority with urgency—like pretending to be an angry boss demanding immediate action. Many employees won't take the time to question such requests if they fear reprimand.

Even the best security systems can be rendered useless by a single mistake—like an employee who shares a password over the phone or clicks on a malicious link. That's why social engineering is often the **first stage** in a larger attack. Once the attacker gains entry, they can escalate their access, install malware, or steal data.

To defend against social engineering, both awareness and skepticism are essential. Here are some **key prevention tips**:

- **Verify Identities**: Always confirm a person's identity through a second method. If someone calls claiming to be from IT, hang up and call the department back using a known internal number.
- **Slow Down**: Social engineers thrive on urgency. Take a moment to assess the situation. Question any request that seems out of the ordinary.
- **Limit Information Sharing**: Be cautious about what you share on social media or over the phone. Even small details can be used to craft believable attacks.
- **Use Security Protocols**: Organizations should implement policies that require multi-step verification before sensitive actions are taken, such as transferring money or changing passwords.
- **Educate and Train Regularly**: Ongoing security awareness training is critical. Simulated phishing and impersonation tests can help reinforce good habits.

- **Report Suspicious Behavior**: Encourage a culture where employees feel comfortable reporting anything unusual, even if they're not sure it's a threat.

Ultimately, the strongest defense against social engineering is a **healthy sense of doubt**. In a world where attackers pose as trusted insiders, it's better to verify twice than to trust blindly once.

The human brain is the most complex and powerful processor in the world—but it's also the most exploitable. Hackers know that. And unless we train ourselves to think like defenders, we'll keep falling into their traps.

In the next chapter, we'll dive into the technical side of cybercrime: **malware, ransomware, and spyware**—what they are, how they work, and how to stop them before they take over your system.

Jessica's wire transfer story

Jessica Alvarez was proud of her job. As an executive assistant at a growing healthcare startup in Miami, she was the gatekeeper—coordinating meetings, screening emails, managing calendars. She prided herself on being fast, responsive, and reliable. But one Friday morning, she became the center of a cybercrime investigation she never saw coming.

At 10:06 a.m., an email landed in her inbox: **From:** *ceooffice@medicorptx.com* **Subject:** *Confidential – Immediate Wire Transfer Needed*

The message was direct and urgent:

> "Jessica, I need you to process a wire transfer for a vendor we've used in the past. It's time-sensitive. I'm on a call—please don't delay. The account info is below. Confirm once complete. —Derek"

Derek was the CEO. He was traveling that week. The tone was familiar. He often ended messages abruptly when in meetings. Jessica didn't hesitate. She opened the company's banking portal and began entering the wire transfer details for $38,000.

She paused only once—to ask herself if she remembered this particular vendor. But the email had CC'd what looked like Derek's executive assistant, and she assumed it was legitimate. She completed the transfer and replied, "Done."

It took less than ten minutes.

An hour later, the real Derek called from his hotel. "Wire transfer? What are you talking about?" Jessica's face drained of color. It wasn't him. It never was.

A hacker had used **social engineering** to mimic Derek's language, spoof his email, and create just enough urgency to bypass Jessica's normally sharp instincts. He knew she was an assistant. He knew Derek was out of the office. He knew they used wire transfers regularly. How? Social media. LinkedIn. Press releases. And maybe even a prior breach at one of their vendors.

The company filed a report with the FBI. The funds were unrecoverable.

Halfway across the country, a different kind of social engineering attack played out in a hospital waiting room in Phoenix. A young man wearing a security badge walked through a staff-only door without swiping a keycard. He had followed a nurse inside after holding the door politely. No one questioned him.

In his pocket was a USB stick. He found an unattended workstation, plugged it in, and waited three seconds. It ran a script that connected to an external command server. By the time he walked out, a remote backdoor had been established in the hospital's internal network.

Tailgating. One of the oldest, simplest forms of social engineering. And it worked—because people are conditioned to be polite.

Meanwhile, across the Atlantic in the UK, Marcus, a college freshman studying cybersecurity, was running a "reverse social engineering" experiment as part of his class project. He deliberately created an error on a classmate's computer—remotely disabling a print driver using an admin access vulnerability in the school's shared system.

Then he sent a message from a fake tech support account:

> "We've detected an issue on your student account. Please contact the IT Help Desk at extension 4429 for assistance."

Sure enough, the student called. Marcus answered in a calm, professional tone, walked them through a "fix," and had them download a harmless test file. He revealed the ruse later that day—and was applauded by his professor. It had worked flawlessly. Why? Because the victim thought they were initiating the call. They felt in control. That's the genius of **reverse social engineering**.

But outside of classrooms, these techniques had real-world consequences.

In Washington, D.C., a federal employee was tricked by a caller posing as "Internal IT Security." The voice on the line was calm and confident.

> "We've detected suspicious login activity on your federal access account. I just need to confirm your employee ID and security phrase to reauthorize access." Flustered and worried, she gave it to him. Within fifteen minutes, her credentials were used to access sensitive documents, triggering a full system lockdown.

She later confessed, "He didn't sound like a hacker. He sounded like someone who wanted to help."

That's what makes social engineering so powerful. It doesn't look like a threat. It looks like your boss, your IT team, a helpful stranger, or a colleague doing their job. It doesn't crash systems or break firewalls. It slips past them, wearing a mask of normalcy.

Jessica, the executive assistant, still replayed that Friday morning in her head. The email. The tone. The speed with which she acted. Her company revised its payment protocols afterward: no more financial requests via email without verbal confirmation. But the money was gone, and so was a bit of her confidence.

She wasn't stupid. She was human.

And in the world of social engineering, that's all the opening an attacker needs.

Chapter 4: Malware, Ransomware, and Spyware Explained

Malware, short for *malicious software*, is any program or code designed to infiltrate, damage, disrupt, or gain unauthorized access to a computer system. While the term is often thrown around in tech circles, many people don't fully understand just how sophisticated—and dangerous—today's malware has become. It's no longer limited to sketchy popups or outdated antivirus threats. Malware is now the engine behind everything from ransomware attacks that shut down hospitals to spyware that silently watches your every move.

There are many **types of malware**, each with a distinct function, method of infection, and goal. Let's break down the most common categories you need to understand:

1. Viruses

Viruses are the oldest and most well-known type of malware. They attach themselves to legitimate files and replicate when those files are shared or opened. Once active, they can corrupt files, delete data, slow down systems, or even render a device unusable. Viruses require user interaction to spread, such as opening an infected document or running a compromised application.

2. Worms

Unlike viruses, worms do not require user interaction. They spread automatically across networks by exploiting system vulnerabilities. A worm can infect an entire office—or even global networks—without anyone clicking anything. Worms often cause network congestion, slowdowns, or system crashes.

3. Trojans

Named after the infamous Trojan Horse of Greek mythology, Trojans disguise themselves as harmless or beneficial software. They trick users into installing them, and once inside, they may open backdoors for remote access, steal data, or install other forms of malware.

4. Ransomware

This particularly destructive form of malware encrypts your files or locks your system, then demands a ransom payment to restore access. Victims are often told to pay in cryptocurrency within a short timeframe—or risk permanent data loss. Ransomware attacks have affected individuals, schools, corporations, and even city governments.

5. Spyware

Spyware is designed to secretly monitor your activities. It can track keystrokes, capture passwords, watch emails, and record browsing history. Some advanced spyware can even activate webcams or microphones without your knowledge. It's often used in corporate espionage or identity theft.

6. Adware

While not always malicious, adware is a form of malware that bombards users with unwanted ads. Some adware tracks user behavior and redirects web traffic to malicious websites. Although annoying rather than destructive, adware can slow your device and open the door to more serious threats.

7. Rootkits and Keyloggers

Rootkits are tools that allow hackers to gain and maintain administrator-level access to a system without detection. Keyloggers secretly record keystrokes, capturing sensitive data like passwords and credit card numbers.

How Malware Infects Systems

Malware doesn't just "show up." It needs a way in. The most common **infection vectors** include:

- **Email attachments and links** (especially from phishing emails)

- **Infected downloads** from untrustworthy websites or pirated software
- **Compromised websites** with drive-by downloads that install malware when you visit the site
- **USB devices** (infected flash drives or external drives)
- **Fake updates** or pop-up alerts that prompt users to download malware disguised as legitimate software
- **Malicious ads** (known as malvertising) that automatically infect users when displayed on websites

Once installed, malware can perform a wide range of malicious activities: stealing credentials, deleting files, hijacking your computer for cryptocurrency mining, recording your private conversations, or encrypting your entire hard drive.

What Ransomware Looks Like in Action

A typical ransomware attack starts with a phishing email that tricks the user into clicking a link or downloading an infected file. That file installs ransomware in the background. Within minutes, it encrypts important files—documents, photos, spreadsheets, databases—and replaces them with unreadable gibberish.

The victim is then shown a ransom note on their screen:

> "Your files have been encrypted. To restore access, send 0.5 Bitcoin to this wallet address within 72 hours. Failure to do so will result in permanent deletion of your data."

The pressure is psychological. Victims feel helpless, especially if backups were not in place. Paying the ransom doesn't always guarantee file recovery. In some cases, the files are never returned—or the system is left infected anyway.

Why Spyware Is So Dangerous

Spyware is dangerous because it operates silently. You may never know it's there—until your identity is stolen or your accounts are drained. It often arrives bundled with free software, browser extensions, or mobile apps. Advanced spyware can log your activity for months without detection.

Corporate spies, jealous partners, and cybercriminals have all used spyware to surveil targets. It's especially dangerous on mobile devices, where users store personal data, photos, and real-time location.

How to Detect and Remove Malware

Malware detection isn't always obvious. Warning signs include:

- Sluggish system performance
- Pop-up ads, even when not browsing
- New programs or icons you don't recognize
- Redirected browser searches
- Webcam or microphone light turning on unexpectedly
- Unusual network activity

If you suspect malware, take these steps:

1. **Disconnect from the Internet** to prevent further data transmission.
2. **Run a full system scan** using a reputable antivirus or anti-malware tool like Malwarebytes, Bitdefender, or Norton.
3. **Delete any quarantined or flagged files.**
4. **Update your operating system and security patches.**
5. **Reset passwords** on all important accounts.

6. **Restore from a clean backup** if necessary.

In extreme cases, wiping the entire system and reinstalling the operating system may be required to fully remove the threat.

How to Prevent Malware Infections

An ounce of prevention is worth a terabyte of cure. Follow these essential practices to stay protected:

- **Keep all software updated** (especially your operating system and browser)
- **Use a strong antivirus program** with real-time scanning
- **Avoid clicking on links or attachments in unsolicited emails**
- **Only download software from trusted sources**
- **Avoid pirated software or cracked programs**
- **Use firewalls and VPNs** for additional layers of defense
- **Backup important files regularly** to an external drive or secure cloud service

- **Use browser extensions that block malicious ads and trackers**

Malware isn't just a nuisance—it's a tool of extortion, theft, and surveillance. It's evolving constantly, and the only way to defend against it is to stay informed, stay cautious, and build smart habits into your daily tech use.

In the next chapter, we'll look at **real-world scams** and breakdown how hackers have used these tactics to steal millions from businesses and individuals around the world—sometimes in ways you'd never expect.

It started with a spreadsheet.

Carla Jensen, a small business owner in Minneapolis, had just received an email from what looked like a longtime supplier. The subject line read: **Updated Pricing Sheet – Urgent**. The timing made sense—she had just reached out the week before asking about inventory costs. So when she saw the Excel file attachment, she clicked.

Nothing happened. The file seemed blank.

She shrugged and closed it. But in the background, something very real had just taken root.

Carla's computer was now infected with **ransomware**—a variant that slowly spread through her network, silently encrypting documents, customer records, invoices, and even her accounting software. She didn't notice anything wrong until the next morning, when every file she opened was replaced by gibberish and a single message glared across her desktop:

> "Your files have been encrypted. Pay 0.4 Bitcoin within 72 hours or your data will be permanently lost."

She gasped. Years of data—gone. No backups. No cloud sync. Everything her business relied on was now locked in a digital vault. Frantically, she called her IT contractor, but he confirmed what she feared. The infection had hit every device on her network. Her only options were to pay the ransom or start over from scratch.

Carla chose to pay.

Within hours of transferring the funds, she received a decryption key. Some of the files were restored. Others weren't. A few remained corrupted. And as she rebooted her system, a chill ran down her spine—was the malware really gone? Or was the attacker still watching?

Meanwhile, across the country in San Diego, 17-year-old Devonte Ramirez was tinkering with his new laptop. He'd downloaded a free screen-recording app to create gaming tutorials for his YouTube channel. The site had offered glowing reviews and thousands of downloads. But hidden inside the installer was **spyware**—a keylogger that silently recorded every keystroke, screenshot, and login attempt.

Within a week, Devonte's Instagram and Gmail were hacked. His passwords had been sent to a command server in Eastern Europe, and someone began posting scam ads through his social media. He was locked out of his accounts and confused about how it had even happened—until a local cybersecurity volunteer at a school event scanned his device and showed him the infection.

"You didn't do anything wrong," the expert said gently. "You just trusted the wrong download."

Devonte felt violated. Someone had been watching everything—his messages, his DMs, maybe even his webcam.

At a law office in Boston, attorney Lisa Mendelson faced a different kind of malware. Her entire system had slowed to a crawl. Pop-up ads appeared even when no browser was open. Her search engine kept redirecting to unfamiliar sites, and her desktop had strange icons she hadn't installed. It wasn't ransomware or spyware—but **adware**, flooding her system with junk.

The adware had come bundled with a free PDF converter she'd downloaded last month.

"What's the harm in that?" she'd thought at the time. Now, she realized it had opened the door to more malicious activity. Her antivirus software had failed to detect it, and every time she tried to remove it, the programs returned after reboot.

Her firm's IT team eventually had to do a full system reset to wipe the infection.

Then there was **Tom**, a logistics manager at a freight company in Houston. He never downloaded suspicious files. He avoided strange links. But he made one small mistake—he plugged in a free USB drive handed out at a conference.

The drive contained a trojan.

Unbeknownst to him, it created a backdoor into his company's network. Over the next two weeks, hackers used that door to gather data on delivery routes, client invoices, and even customer credit card details. They didn't trigger alarms. They just quietly siphoned data—until one day, customers began reporting fraudulent charges.

By the time the breach was discovered, it had cost the company over $300,000 in regulatory fines, reputation damage, and lost business.

All these stories had one thing in common: malware didn't knock down the door—it was invited in.

Whether through a fake invoice, a free app, a USB giveaway, or a bundled file, malware thrives on trust, curiosity, and convenience. It hides in plain sight, waiting for a single click, tap, or download to take control.

Carla never got all her files back. Devonte had to rebuild his online presence from scratch. Lisa learned to avoid anything that wasn't from a verified source. Tom's company implemented new protocols: no unknown USBs, no unverified software, and mandatory security training for all employees.

And yet, across the world, hundreds of new malware strains are created every day. Some are crude. Others are incredibly advanced—capable of evading detection, spreading laterally across networks, and extracting data with surgical precision.

The lesson? If you use a device connected to the internet, you are a target. Not because of who you are, but because of what your system represents: access, data, and leverage.

But being a target doesn't mean being a victim.

Learn the signs. Stay alert. And never assume that silence means safety—because the most dangerous malware is the kind you never see coming.

Chapter 5: Real-World Scams That Cost Millions

Cybercrime is no longer a theoretical threat reserved for hackers in Hollywood movies. It is a very real, rapidly growing industry costing the global economy hundreds of billions of dollars every year. Behind every phishing email, fake login screen, or ransomware message is a deliberate, financially motivated attack that can cripple businesses, drain personal savings, or even shut down entire governments.

In this chapter, we'll examine real-world scams that caused massive financial damage and the key takeaways you need to protect yourself from suffering the same fate. Each case offers a cautionary tale and exposes how common the tactics are—regardless of industry, geography, or company size.

1. The $100 Million Phishing Scam Against Google and Facebook

Between 2013 and 2015, two of the world's largest tech giants—Google and Facebook—were defrauded out of over $100 million by one man using a **simple email scam**.

Evaldas Rimasauskas, a Lithuanian national, posed as a legitimate Asian-based vendor. He created fake email addresses, invoices, and contracts that closely mimicked a real hardware supplier used by both companies. He sent fake invoices to employees in the accounts payable departments, and they paid—thinking they were legitimate bills for real services.

The scam worked for years before being detected.

Lesson: Even large companies with professional accounting teams can be fooled if verification steps are skipped. Always confirm payment requests through multiple channels.

2. The Colonial Pipeline Ransomware Attack

In May 2021, a ransomware group called DarkSide targeted the Colonial Pipeline, the largest fuel pipeline system in the United States. The attackers infiltrated the network through a compromised password on a VPN account and deployed ransomware that forced the company to shut down operations for several days.

The result? Fuel shortages, price spikes, and panic-buying across the East Coast. Colonial Pipeline ultimately paid the hackers **$4.4 million** in Bitcoin to regain control of their systems.

Lesson: Even critical infrastructure is vulnerable to weak passwords and poor authentication. The attack wasn't highly technical—it was about exploiting low-hanging vulnerabilities.

3. Barbara Corcoran's Assistant Sends $400,000 to Fraudsters

In 2020, Barbara Corcoran, the real estate mogul and "Shark Tank" investor, lost nearly **$400,000** in a business email compromise (BEC) scam.

Cybercriminals impersonated her assistant and sent an email to her bookkeeper requesting a wire transfer for a property renovation. The email address was nearly identical to the assistant's real one—except for one extra letter. The bookkeeper complied, and the funds were gone.

Lesson: A single character in an email address can make or break a scam. Always confirm unusual financial requests by phone or face-to-face, especially when they involve large sums.

4. The Hospital That Paid to Save Lives

In 2017, a small hospital in Indiana was hit with a ransomware attack that encrypted critical medical systems and locked out healthcare professionals from patient records.

With no backups in place and patient lives on the line, the hospital made the decision to pay the ransom—around **$55,000** in Bitcoin—to restore access.

The systems were decrypted, but the incident highlighted the dangerous intersection of healthcare and cybersecurity.

Lesson: Failing to prepare a backup strategy can turn ransomware from an inconvenience into a life-threatening emergency. Hospitals, schools, and municipal agencies are often under-protected targets.

5. The $17 Million "Fake CEO" Scam

A company in Austria was manipulated into transferring **€17 million** to a foreign account after receiving a phone call from someone pretending to be the company's CEO.

This scam combined **social engineering** with deep research. The scammers knew the CEO's travel schedule and created a convincing voice and email narrative that instructed the finance department to make the wire transfer immediately.

The finance employee complied—and by the time the real CEO returned, the money had vanished into offshore accounts.

Lesson: Authority and urgency are powerful manipulation tools. Employees should be trained to question even executive-level requests that fall outside normal procedures.

Common Themes in These Scams

Although the dollar amounts vary, all of these attacks share a few key characteristics:

1. **They exploit trust.** Scammers know how to sound legitimate. They imitate coworkers, executives, vendors, and even family members to lower your defenses.

2. **They rely on urgency.** Many of these scams created pressure to act fast—before the target had time to think critically or verify the request.

3. **They bypass technology.** Even companies with strong firewalls, antivirus programs, and intrusion detection systems were compromised—because the attackers went after the people, not the machines.

4. **They were preventable.** In most cases, a simple verification step, a second phone call, or stronger employee training could have stopped the attack.

How to Protect Yourself and Your Organization

If these scams can happen to billion-dollar companies, they can happen to anyone. But there are practical steps you can take to dramatically reduce your risk:

- **Use Multi-Factor Authentication (MFA):** A stolen password is far less dangerous when an attacker also needs a second code or token to access an account.

- **Verify Payment Requests:** Never authorize wire

transfers or sensitive changes without verbal confirmation or a secondary approval process.

- **Conduct Regular Security Training:** Employees are the first line of defense. Teach them how to recognize phishing emails, suspicious links, and urgent fraud tactics.

- **Use Domain Monitoring and Email Filtering:** Block or flag lookalike domains and unusual sender patterns. Use SPF, DKIM, and DMARC to protect outgoing emails.

- **Back Up Everything:** Create automated, secure backups of critical systems. Test them regularly and store them offline to protect against ransomware.

- **Have a Response Plan:** Know who to contact and what to do in the event of a cyberattack. Speed and clarity during a crisis can mean the difference between containment and catastrophe.

The most dangerous cyberattacks aren't always the most technical—they're the most believable. Fraudsters know how to mimic reality, leverage authority, and create emotional pressure. Your best defense is awareness, systems that promote double-checking, and a culture that encourages smart skepticism.

In the next chapter, we'll pull back the curtain on the tools hackers use—keyloggers, spoofing software, fake Wi-Fi networks, and more—and show how even simple software can lead to devastating breaches when it's in the wrong hands.

Your network has been seized story

The email looked legitimate. It came from the CEO's personal assistant, included the company's official logo, and referenced an ongoing project the finance team had been discussing for weeks. There was nothing suspicious about it—at least, that's what Lisa Cheng thought as she forwarded the $247,000 wire request to her supervisor for approval.

She'd been at the company for six years, working in accounts payable, and had processed dozens of transfers just like this one. The request included all the correct terminology, formatted according to internal protocol, and even carried the CEO's digital signature.

Three days later, her stomach dropped.

Her boss, the CFO, walked into her office pale and wide-eyed. "Lisa," he said quietly, "that vendor payment you processed on Monday—Derek never sent it."

The money was gone.

As the investigation unfolded, Lisa learned the truth. Hackers had used **email spoofing** to impersonate the CEO's assistant. They studied internal communications, learned project timelines from LinkedIn and press releases, and timed their attack perfectly. It wasn't random—it was **targeted**, **researched**, and **scalpel-precise**.

The company never recovered the funds. The bank said the transfer was authorized. Law enforcement had little to trace—the offshore account vanished after 24 hours. Lisa wasn't fired, but she never quite recovered from the shock. She'd done everything right—except pause to verify.

Meanwhile, 600 miles away, a ransomware attack was unfolding at a school district in Ohio. Superintendent Daniel Grady arrived at work to find dozens of teachers locked out of their systems. Every file—lesson plans, student records, payroll data—was encrypted.

On the screen was a message:

> "Your network has been seized. Pay 3.2 Bitcoin within 72 hours or your files will be destroyed."

The IT team traced the breach to a single staff laptop. The culprit? A phishing email that disguised itself as a professional development webinar registration. A teacher had downloaded the attachment. One click had infected the entire district.

Daniel knew they didn't have clean backups. Paying was their only shot. The district board approved the ransom. Within 48 hours, they paid over $90,000 in Bitcoin—and waited.

The hackers delivered the decryption key. Some files came back. Others were permanently lost. The district faced public scrutiny, lawsuits, and months of disruption.

Elsewhere in Los Angeles, a different kind of scam played out—not ransomware, not phishing, but **impersonation**.

It began with a phone call to a high-ranking executive assistant at a biotech firm. The caller claimed to be from their corporate law firm.

"We need to move quickly on a pending acquisition," he said. "Your CEO authorized this wire transfer—everything is urgent, but discreet. Legal teams are copied in. I'll email the documents for your review."

The assistant received the email minutes later. Legal-looking PDFs. NDA clauses. Even encrypted file links. The email domain was nearly identical to the firm's law partner.

She forwarded everything to the CFO. Within an hour, $1.4

million had been wired to what everyone believed was a trusted account. It wasn't. By the time the real law firm responded to the "thank you" email in confusion, the scammers had cashed out the funds and disappeared.

The attack used a technique called **deep spoofing**, where the attackers mimic trusted professionals by copying real names, emails, and workflows. It wasn't hacking—**it was deception perfected**.

Meanwhile, in a quiet suburb in Florida, 68-year-old James Monroe lost his life savings in a cryptocurrency scam. It began on social media. A supposed financial advisor invited him to join a private investment group. He was shown fake dashboards, screenshots of profits, and testimonials from people "just like him."

All it took was one transfer of $10,000 into a so-called crypto wallet. Then another. And another. Within months, he'd lost over $150,000—his retirement fund gone. When he tried to withdraw, the system suddenly asked for more verification fees, withdrawal taxes, and identity proof payments. He realized too late it was all fake.

James reported the scam, but the "company" was based overseas and untraceable. He went public with his story to warn others. "They made me feel like I belonged," he said.

"Like I was going to be wealthy. They used my hope against me."

Across all of these stories—whether involving companies, schools, or individuals—the pattern is clear. Hackers and scammers don't just exploit systems. **They exploit belief.**

They rely on employees assuming emails are real. On staff trusting phone calls. On people being too busy or embarrassed to ask questions. The scams don't succeed because victims are stupid—they succeed because they're human.

What Lisa, Daniel, James, and the biotech executive assistant all had in common was a moment of trust that cost them dearly. But each story also left behind lessons:

Double-check. Verify independently. Question urgency. Don't rely solely on digital cues. And above all—train your team to recognize manipulation before it costs millions.

Because in the world of cybercrime, one moment of inattention is all it takes to become the next story.

Chapter 6: The Tools Hackers Use

Understanding the tools hackers use is a vital part of cybersecurity awareness. Many people assume that hacking is about writing complex code from scratch or having elite technical skills. But in reality, many of today's most devastating cyberattacks are executed with tools that are easily available—some even for free—online.

These tools are created and shared across forums, marketplaces, and encrypted chat groups, and are often packaged in user-friendly interfaces. That means even amateur hackers or "script kiddies" can deploy advanced attacks with little effort. Let's explore some of the most common and powerful tools hackers use—and how they work.

1. Keyloggers

Keyloggers are programs or hardware devices that record every keystroke a user types. They capture passwords, credit card numbers, messages, and any other typed input. Some keyloggers can even record screenshots and clipboard content.

There are two types:

- **Software keyloggers**, which are hidden in malware or trojans

- **Hardware keyloggers**, which are small USB devices secretly attached to a computer

Once installed, keyloggers silently transmit data to the attacker, often without being detected by antivirus software.

2. Remote Access Trojans (RATs)

RATs are a type of malware that gives attackers remote control over an infected device. Once installed, a RAT can:

- Browse files
- Turn on the webcam or microphone
- Log keystrokes
- Take screenshots
- Install or delete software

Hackers use RATs to spy, steal data, or stage a larger attack from the infected system. RATs are often disguised as legitimate files—such as games, apps, or PDFs—and are installed through phishing emails or fake downloads.

3. Packet Sniffers

A packet sniffer captures network traffic in real time. Hackers use them to intercept data like usernames, passwords, and unencrypted emails as they travel across a network. On unsecured public Wi-Fi networks, packet sniffers can harvest data from everyone connected.

Popular tools like **Wireshark** (used by both security experts and attackers) allow users to analyze network packets and reconstruct communication sessions, such as logins or website visits.

4. Spoofing Tools

Spoofing tools allow hackers to impersonate trusted sources. They're used to:

- **Spoof IP addresses**, making it look like traffic is coming from somewhere else
- **Spoof emails**, making messages appear to be from someone inside your organization
- **Spoof websites**, replicating login pages to trick users into entering their credentials

With a well-crafted spoofing tool, attackers can manipulate digital environments and gain trust from unsuspecting victims.

5. Password Cracking Tools

Password cracking tools use various techniques to gain

unauthorized access to accounts. Some of the most common types include:

- **Brute force attacks**: Tries every possible combination of characters
- **Dictionary attacks**: Uses known passwords or variations from password lists
- **Rainbow tables**: Uses precomputed hashes to quickly crack encrypted passwords

Popular tools include **John the Ripper**, **Hydra**, and **Hashcat**. Many of these are used by penetration testers ethically—but they're also widely exploited by criminals.

6. Phishing Kits

Phishing kits are pre-built packages that allow attackers to create convincing phishing websites in minutes. These kits often include:

- A clone of a real website login page
- Scripts to capture credentials and forward them to the attacker
- URL obfuscation tools to mask the true destination

Sold on dark web forums or even shared on Telegram groups, these kits allow low-skilled users to conduct high-impact phishing attacks.

7. Fake Wi-Fi Networks (Evil Twin Attacks)

In an Evil Twin attack, hackers set up a rogue Wi-Fi network that mimics a real one—often using the same name (SSID) as a trusted coffee shop, airport, or hotel network.

Once connected, users' traffic is routed through the hacker's device, allowing them to intercept logins, monitor activity, or redirect users to fake websites. Tools like **Airbase-ng** and **WiFi Pumpkin** are commonly used for this.

8. Exploit Kits

Exploit kits are toolsets designed to find and exploit vulnerabilities in a user's system. When a user visits a compromised website, the kit scans their browser, plugins, and system for weaknesses—such as outdated Java or Flash installations. If a vulnerability is found, it's exploited to install malware automatically.

These kits are sold on cybercrime marketplaces, sometimes bundled with support and tutorials, making them a popular weapon for even novice hackers.

9. Botnets

Botnets are networks of infected devices—computers, servers, or even smart home devices—that are controlled by a hacker. These "zombie" machines are used to:

- Launch Distributed Denial-of-Service (DDoS) attacks
- Send spam or phishing emails
- Steal data in bulk
- Distribute ransomware

Some of the world's largest botnets include millions of devices, many of which are owned by people unaware their machines are compromised.

10. Dark Web Marketplaces

While not tools themselves, dark web markets facilitate the trade of hacking tools, stolen credentials, and services. Hackers can buy:

- Password dumps from previous data breaches
- Ransomware-as-a-Service (RaaS) kits
- Access to compromised email or cloud accounts

- Fake IDs and forged documents

These platforms operate like eBay for criminals, complete with seller reviews, customer service, and escrow payments in cryptocurrency.

Staying Protected Against Hacker Tools

You don't need to understand every line of code, but you do need to recognize how these tools are used—and how to defend against them:

- **Keep all software and systems updated**—many attacks rely on known vulnerabilities
- **Use endpoint protection tools** with behavioral analysis, not just signature detection
- **Avoid public Wi-Fi** without a VPN, and never enter sensitive information on unsecured networks
- **Educate employees** about phishing, spoofing, and suspicious behavior
- **Use strong, unique passwords** with a password manager and enable multi-factor authentication

Hackers are increasingly relying on automation, convenience, and stolen tools to scale their attacks. It's no longer about whether a person is personally targeted—it's about whether they're vulnerable.

In the next chapter, we'll move from tools to tactics—specifically, **how to defend against common attacks**, including the practical, everyday habits that make you harder to hack and less likely to fall for scams or social engineering.

Megan's remote access trojan story

The office looked just like any other: rows of desks, glowing monitors, the hum of conversation. But one workstation, in the back corner of a Chicago marketing firm, had become the unwitting launchpad for a cyberattack. And it all started with an email attachment named *ClientProposal2024.pdf.exe*.

Megan, the firm's junior designer, had received the file from what appeared to be a potential client. The message was polite, well-written, and referenced a recent social media ad campaign. "We loved your last project," it read. "We'd like a proposal for something similar. Please review the attached creative brief."

She clicked. Nothing opened.

She thought nothing of it and went back to work.

What she didn't know was that the file had installed a **Remote Access Trojan (RAT)**—a hidden backdoor that gave a hacker named Ludo, sitting in a shared apartment in Romania, full access to her machine. Through the RAT, he could see her screen, browse files, install programs, and even activate the webcam.

Ludo wasn't interested in Megan's design work. He wanted **credentials**—and her computer had plenty. Saved logins to Slack, cloud storage, and the firm's internal project management system. He quietly exfiltrated everything over the course of an hour. Then he dug deeper, moving laterally through the network.

By the next day, Ludo had access to multiple employee machines. His toolkit included a **keylogger**, silently recording every keystroke, capturing admin passwords and personal data alike. He used a **spoofed internal email** to send a message to the company's financial controller, pretending to be the CEO:

> "Please process the vendor payment today. Here's the updated invoice. Let me know when it's done."

The invoice had been generated using another stolen tool—**a phishing kit** complete with the company's real logo, layout, and tone. The email address looked legitimate, down to a single swapped character.

When the controller clicked the link to “confirm payment,” she landed on what looked like the internal vendor portal. She logged in. Her credentials were captured in real-time.

Ludo now had full access to the company’s financial backend.

Meanwhile, in another part of the world, at a conference in San Francisco, an ambitious cybersecurity student named Troy was demonstrating an **Evil Twin Wi-Fi attack**. He had set up a rogue hotspot named “Conf2024-FreeWiFi” using nothing more than a laptop and a portable router. Dozens of attendees connected to it without thinking—checking emails, logging into bank apps, booking rides.

Troy wasn’t trying to steal anything. His point was simple: **people trust names**, especially when under pressure or in public. Using a **packet sniffer** called Wireshark, he showed how easily usernames and passwords could be intercepted from those using unencrypted sites. He ended his session with a warning: “If you wouldn’t whisper your bank password in a crowded airport, don’t type it into your phone on public Wi-Fi.”

Back in Chicago, the marketing firm's IT admin finally noticed strange activity: an unfamiliar IP accessing their systems from Europe. Passwords were being changed, files deleted. They pulled the plug—literally—and began forensic analysis.

The breach had lasted four days. It had started with one click. The total cost of recovery, system audits, and client trust repair: over $380,000.

Megan was devastated. "I thought it was just a file," she said. "It didn't even open. I had no idea someone could take over my computer like that."

She wasn't alone.

Around the world, hackers used **password cracking tools** to break into accounts with weak logins. A small real estate firm in Nevada had 12 employees using "Welcome123" as their company-wide password—easily cracked in minutes with **dictionary attacks** using tools like John the Ripper.

In another case, a group of cybercriminals bought access to a **botnet** of infected smart home devices—thermostats, cameras, even baby monitors—to stage a massive DDoS attack that took down an entire web hosting company for 6 hours.

And on dark web marketplaces, criminals offered everything from **spyware packages** to pre-configured **ransomware**

kits—complete with 24/7 "tech support" and customization options. It was hacking as a service. And business was booming.

But amid the chaos, awareness was growing.

After the Chicago incident, Megan's firm implemented strict software download policies. They deployed email filters that flagged executable files, banned unsanctioned cloud tools, and required employee training every quarter. VPNs became mandatory for remote work. All accounts had to use multi-factor authentication. The cost of that education had been high—but they weren't going to pay it twice.

The tools hackers use are powerful—but they rely on something even more important: your **permission**, your **click**, your **assumption** that everything is safe.

But once you understand what they use and how they use it, that illusion breaks. You begin to see the threats coming. You pause before clicking. You question the familiar. You become the kind of user who doesn't just rely on software to keep you safe—you become your own firewall.

Chapter 7: How to Protect Yourself from Common Attacks

Now that you've seen how hackers think, the tools they use, and the damage they can cause, it's time to focus on **defense**. The truth is, most cyberattacks are preventable—not through complex software or expensive hardware, but through **consistent habits** and **simple layers of protection** that drastically reduce your vulnerability.

Cybersecurity isn't just for IT professionals. If you own a smartphone, use a laptop, have an email address, or manage social media—you are a potential target. But with the right knowledge and behavior, you can make yourself a hard target. Let's break down how.

1. Use Strong, Unique Passwords

The majority of successful hacks still begin with compromised or reused passwords. Most people reuse the same login credentials across multiple platforms. If just one of those platforms is breached, attackers can test that email-password combo on hundreds of other sites.

Best Practices:

- Use **long passphrases** (12+ characters) that are easy

to remember but hard to guess. Example: SunsetsAreBeautiful!2025

- Avoid common phrases, names, or predictable substitutions (like "P@ssw0rd")
- Never reuse passwords across accounts
- Use a **password manager** (like 1Password, Bitwarden, or Dashlane) to generate and store unique logins securely

2. Enable Multi-Factor Authentication (MFA)

MFA adds an additional layer of protection by requiring something you **know** (your password) and something you **have** (like a smartphone authentication app or SMS code). Even if a hacker gets your password, they still need that second factor to gain access.

Use MFA on:

- Email
- Banking apps
- Cloud storage (Google Drive, Dropbox, etc.)
- Social media

- Work platforms (like Microsoft 365 or Slack)

Apps like **Authy**, **Google Authenticator**, or **Duo** are more secure than SMS, which can be intercepted.

3. Recognize Phishing and Social Engineering Attempts

Hackers rarely "break in"—they're often **invited in**. Phishing, fake login pages, urgent emails, or phone calls pretending to be tech support are all common methods of gaining access.

Always ask yourself:

- Do I know this sender?
- Am I being rushed or pressured?
- Is this link leading to a legitimate site (hover to check)?
- Is the domain spelled correctly?

Never:

- Click links or open attachments in suspicious messages
- Provide passwords or sensitive info via email
- Call back unknown numbers without verifying

When in doubt, contact the person or company directly through an official channel.

4. Keep Software and Devices Updated

Outdated software is a playground for hackers. They target vulnerabilities in old versions of apps, operating systems, and plugins.

Tips:

- Turn on **automatic updates** for your OS, browser, and antivirus
- Regularly update mobile apps—especially banking, messaging, and email
- Uninstall apps or extensions you no longer use
- Replace unsupported devices or systems

Security patches are released frequently for a reason. Don't delay them.

5. Back Up Your Data Regularly

Backups are your lifeline if ransomware hits or your device crashes.

How to Back Up Safely:

- Use **cloud services** (Google Drive, iCloud, OneDrive) with encryption
- Have a **local backup** on an external hard drive stored offline
- Automate backups on a weekly or daily basis
- Test backups periodically to make sure they restore properly

If your files are encrypted by ransomware and you have a clean backup, you won't need to pay a ransom to recover them.

6. Use Antivirus and Anti-Malware Tools

These tools help detect, quarantine, and remove known threats.

Look for tools with:

- Real-time scanning
- Web filtering
- Email scanning
- Behavior-based detection (not just signature matching)

Some trusted options include **Bitdefender**, **Norton**, **ESET**, **Kaspersky**, and **Malwarebytes**. Always download software from official websites.

7. Be Cautious With Wi-Fi Networks

Public Wi-Fi is a hacker's dream. Open networks in airports, cafes, and hotels can be spoofed or monitored easily.

Safe Practices:

- Use a **VPN** (Virtual Private Network) when connecting to public Wi-Fi
- Avoid logging into sensitive accounts while on public networks
- Turn off "auto-connect" on your device for unknown networks
- Prefer using your phone's hotspot when possible

VPNs encrypt your data, shielding it from eavesdropping—even on unsecured networks.

8. Educate Yourself and Others

Cybersecurity isn't one-and-done. It's ongoing. Hackers constantly evolve, so your awareness must as well.

Suggestions:

- Follow cybersecurity news (Krebs on Security, ThreatPost, The Hacker News)
- Take periodic online training courses
- Encourage friends, family, or staff to learn the basics
- Conduct simulated phishing tests for your team

The more you know, the better you can respond when something doesn't feel right.

9. Watch for Warning Signs of a Breach

Sometimes, subtle clues can reveal a breach in progress.

Red Flags:

- Unexplained device slowdown
- Strange pop-ups or browser redirects
- Unusual account activity or password resets
- Antivirus turning off by itself
- New apps or icons appearing without your action

If you notice these signs:

- Disconnect from the internet
- Run a full antivirus scan
- Change passwords from a clean device
- Alert your IT team or service provider

10. Secure Your Physical Devices

Cybersecurity isn't just digital—it starts with physical control.

Steps to take:

- Use device passwords or biometric locks (fingerprint/Face ID)
- Set devices to auto-lock after a short period of inactivity
- Never leave devices unattended in public spaces
- Use remote wipe features for lost phones or laptops (Find My iPhone, Android Device Manager)

A stolen phone or laptop without encryption or a lock screen is an open door.

Ultimately, cyber defense is about **building habits**, not just installing tools. No one is immune, but everyone can become more resilient. If you apply even half of the practices in this chapter, you'll be better protected than the vast majority of people online.

In the next chapter, we'll discuss **exactly what to do if you've been hacked**—how to respond, recover, and prevent further damage when things go wrong.

Jillian's story

Jillian was exhausted.

She'd just wrapped up a 12-hour day running her online boutique and was about to shut her laptop when she saw the email: **"Amazon Security: Suspicious activity detected on your account. Immediate action required."**

She clicked without thinking. The page looked exactly like Amazon's login portal. Her heart raced—she couldn't afford to have her storefront or payment settings compromised.

She entered her credentials. The page refreshed... and redirected to the real Amazon homepage.

At first, she assumed it was just a glitch. But an hour later, her Gmail, PayPal, and Instagram were all locked. Her phone buzzed with verification codes she hadn't requested. And her online store dashboard—where she processed customer orders—suddenly showed a blank balance.

Jillian had just been phished. And the dominoes were falling fast.

But her story didn't end there.

Three months earlier, her friend Marcus had warned her about cyber threats. He was a freelance IT consultant and had practically begged her to improve her digital hygiene. He even gave her a checklist:

- Set up a password manager
- Enable two-factor authentication
- Back up your shop's database
- Keep software updated
- Never reuse passwords
- Don't click on links in sketchy emails

Jillian had meant to do it. But business was booming, and she never made the time. Until now.

Her heart pounded as she raced to reset her credentials. Thankfully, the hacker had been sloppy. Marcus, who she called in a panic, guided her through the triage. Together, they disconnected her laptop from Wi-Fi, ran a malware scan, and confirmed that her backups—though outdated—hadn't been compromised.

By midnight, she was regaining access to her core accounts. It was messy, but manageable.

That night changed everything.

She spent the next weekend installing a password manager, securing every login with unique, 16-character phrases. She enabled multi-factor authentication on her store, email, and banking platforms. She deleted dozens of unused apps from her phone, and stopped auto-connecting to public Wi-Fi. She also signed up for a VPN subscription and used it any time she accessed customer data or managed payments.

And she made her employees do the same.

Marcus walked her team through phishing simulations—showing them just how realistic scam emails can look. He installed browser extensions to block malicious trackers and ads, and taught them how to hover over links before clicking, how to spot spoofed domains, and how to question anything that felt rushed or "off."

A month later, one of Jillian's assistants received an email from what looked like Shopify, asking to "confirm ownership." It had the logo, her full name, and the right store URL. But something felt off. The sender's domain was "shop1fy.biz." Instead of clicking, she messaged Jillian directly.

"You saved us," Jillian told her, remembering how close she'd come to losing everything.

Elsewhere, in Atlanta, a retired veteran named Harold avoided a ransomware attack just by doing something simple—keeping his system updated. A neighbor sent him a "tax refund calculator" that turned out to be malicious. But Harold's operating system blocked the installation attempt. He had updated Windows the night before, unknowingly patching the vulnerability the malware relied on.

"I didn't even do anything," he told his niece later. "Just followed the update reminders."

That's the power of prevention.

And in a Miami café, 23-year-old graphic designer Tyrese used a VPN on public Wi-Fi without thinking twice. His friends mocked him for being paranoid. But when one of them later had their Dropbox contents wiped after logging in at the same coffee shop, Tyrese didn't say "I told you so." He just helped them install the same protections he used.

The point wasn't to be paranoid. It was to be prepared.

Jillian's story became her lesson—and her mission. She added a "Cyber Safety" checklist to her employee onboarding. She created a monthly backup routine. And she started educating her customers on staying safe while shopping online.

What she realized—and what every character in this chapter learned—is that **protection is rarely dramatic**. It's not about firewalls or hackers in hoodies. It's about habits:

- Pausing before clicking
- Verifying requests
- Using long, unique passwords
- Saying "no" to urgency
- Updating without delay
- Treating digital life as seriously as physical safety

Because in a connected world, your data is your identity. And your identity is worth protecting.

Chapter 8: What to Do If You've Been Hacked

Despite your best efforts, it can still happen. You get hacked. Your screen flashes with an error. Your accounts are suddenly locked. You notice unusual charges, strange emails, or alerts that someone logged in from another country. Your heart races, and the panic sets in: *What now?*

This chapter is about exactly that—how to respond calmly, strategically, and effectively when a breach occurs. Whether it's a personal account, a business system, or a device, acting quickly can make all the difference in containing the damage.

Step 1: Recognize the Signs of a Hack

The first challenge is recognizing that you've been hacked. Some signs are obvious—ransomware messages, account lockouts, or system crashes. Others are subtle and easy to overlook.

Common warning signs include:

- Login notifications from unfamiliar locations or devices
- Passwords no longer working
- Charges on your account you didn't make

- Friends reporting spam messages from you
- Browser redirects or unfamiliar toolbars appearing
- Files disappearing or being encrypted
- Antivirus or firewall turning off without your action

If you notice any of these, it's time to act immediately.

Step 2: Disconnect from the Internet

As soon as you suspect an attack, **disconnect the affected device from Wi-Fi or Ethernet**. This can stop malware from spreading, prevent data from being exfiltrated, and break a hacker's remote control over the device.

If you're on a shared business or home network, disconnect other connected devices as well.

Step 3: Identify What Was Compromised

Take stock of what systems or accounts were affected.

Ask yourself:

- Was it just one account (email, Facebook), or multiple?
- Was it one device (laptop, phone), or a company-wide system?

- Was sensitive data accessed—like banking info, client files, or health records?

Understanding the **scope** of the breach helps determine your next move. Write down a timeline: what you did, when you noticed issues, and what devices or services were involved.

Step 4: Change Passwords—From a Safe Device

Do **not** change passwords on the hacked device if it might be infected with malware or a keylogger. Use a **different, clean device**—like a phone or backup computer—to reset your passwords.

Start with your **primary email account**—since it's usually the recovery key for all others.

Then reset:

- Banking and payment accounts
- Work-related systems
- Cloud storage (Dropbox, Google Drive, iCloud)
- Social media
- Online shopping platforms

Use strong, unique passwords for each account and enable

multi-factor authentication (MFA) wherever possible.

Step 5: Scan and Clean Your Devices

Run a **full system scan** using a reputable antivirus or anti-malware program. If malware is found, follow the software's guidance to quarantine or delete the threat.

In more severe cases, you may need to:

- **Reinstall your operating system** (factory reset)
- **Reformat your drive** from a known-good recovery image
- Seek professional help for data recovery or forensic analysis

After cleaning, reinstall security updates and patches immediately.

Step 6: Check for Data Loss or Theft

Determine if any sensitive files, customer data, or intellectual property were stolen. Review logs, file modification times, and backup comparisons to detect unauthorized access.

If client data or payment information was compromised, you may be legally required to:

- Notify affected parties
- Report the breach to regulators (depending on your country or state)
- Follow compliance procedures (e.g., GDPR, HIPAA, PCI-DSS)

Document everything. Time, nature of the breach, systems affected, and steps taken to fix it.

Step 7: Report the Incident

Depending on the situation, you may need to report the hack to:

- Your **bank or credit card provider** (to stop fraudulent charges)
- Your **employer or IT department**
- A **cybersecurity professional or recovery service**
- Law enforcement or cybercrime units (such as the FBI's Internet Crime Complaint Center at ic3.gov)

Many countries now have dedicated cybercrime agencies or hotlines.

If you're a business, having a clear **incident response plan** makes this much easier. It's worth building one before an attack ever happens.

Step 8: Review and Monitor

Don't assume it's over once you've changed passwords. Hackers may have:

- Planted backdoors or remote-access software
- Stolen credentials you haven't reset
- Gained access to connected systems or backup drives

Take time to:

- Review account activity logs (many platforms show logins, device IPs, etc.)
- Monitor financial accounts daily for the next several weeks
- Set up **alerts** for login attempts or suspicious activity
- Consider freezing your credit with major bureaus if personal identity data was compromised

Step 9: Rebuild With Better Security

Now is the time to harden your defenses.

Post-hack steps include:

- Installing a **password manager** and updating all weak logins
- Implementing **MFA** across every account that supports it
- Creating secure, **offline backups** and testing recovery
- Educating others on what happened—so it doesn't happen again
- Documenting the incident to improve future response

Treat a hack like a fire. You rebuild smarter, with fireproofing and smoke detectors in place.

Final Reminder: Don't Panic—Act Intelligently

Many victims of cyberattacks freeze or make the situation worse by acting rashly—like messaging the hacker, deleting logs, or ignoring the issue entirely.

Stay calm. Act with purpose. Document everything. And get help when needed.

Most importantly, don't feel ashamed. Getting hacked doesn't mean you were careless—it means you're human. But learning from the breach ensures it never happens the same way again.

In the next chapter, we'll walk you through building a **personal cybersecurity plan**—a practical checklist and routine you can use to protect your identity, data, devices, and finances every single day.

Now, lets go over Chloe's instagram story

It started with an Instagram notification.

Chloe Hernandez, a freelance artist with over 40,000 followers, had just finished posting a new collection of watercolor prints when she received an alert: **"Your account has been accessed from a new device in Moscow."**

Her heart sank.

She quickly opened the app—but it was too late. Her profile photo was gone. The bio now had a crypto wallet link. Her content had been deleted. Her email no longer worked with the login. And when she tried to reset her password, the system told her: *This email is not associated with any active account.*

She had been hacked.

At first, Chloe panicked. Her entire business ran through Instagram—her DMs, her commissions, her portfolio. She'd never enabled two-factor authentication. She reused the same password across several platforms. And she hadn't backed up her most recent artwork.

Within ten minutes, she went from business owner to locked-out spectator.

But she didn't freeze for long.

She called her friend Nick, a tech-savvy copywriter who'd experienced a similar attack months earlier. He answered on the first ring. "Okay, breathe," he said. "We're going to work through this."

The first thing they did was isolate the threat. Nick told her to immediately disconnect her laptop and phone from Wi-Fi. "If it's malware-related, we don't want it spreading."

Next, they grabbed Chloe's tablet—a device she hadn't used in weeks and knew was clean. From there, she reset every password she could think of: email, Etsy, banking, Google Drive. Anything connected to her online identity. She used new, unique passwords generated by a password manager Nick helped her install.

Then they ran a malware scan on her laptop. The antivirus tool flagged a suspicious browser extension—a "free shipping calculator" she'd installed last week. It was actually spyware that had logged her credentials and sent them to an external server.

They deleted it immediately.

She emailed Instagram's security team and submitted a stolen account report. While she waited, Nick helped her freeze her credit with Equifax, Experian, and TransUnion, just in case identity info had been compromised. "You don't know what else they grabbed," he said. "Better to get ahead of it."

Chloe was overwhelmed—but she followed every step.

Three days later, Instagram emailed her with good news: her identity had been verified, and her account had been restored. She cried. And then she rebuilt.

This time, she enabled **multi-factor authentication**. She installed real antivirus protection. She backed up all her artwork to cloud and external drives. She created new passwords for every account and stopped using the same login for multiple platforms.

But more than that—she **documented everything**. Every step, every setting, every fix. And she turned it into a blog post that went viral in the art community: *"I Got Hacked—Here's Exactly What I Did to Recover."*

Artists, small business owners, students, and parents began emailing her with their own stories. Chloe replied to every message. "You're not alone," she told them. "It's scary, but you can take control."

Meanwhile, across the country, a gym owner named Andre faced a different kind of breach. One of his employees had reused a weak password for the membership management system. One morning, the system was down. Files were corrupted. And the screen displayed a message: **"Your data has been encrypted. Pay 2 BTC within 72 hours."**

Andre called his IT provider in a panic.

But this time, he had a weapon most victims didn't: **backups**.

The technician wiped the infected system and restored clean versions of all records from a backup taken just 48 hours earlier. The business was back online within the day. Andre never paid the ransom.

Afterward, he implemented a new policy:

- All employees had to complete a cybersecurity training
- Passwords were managed through encrypted vaults

- Backups were now performed daily and stored offline

He framed the ransomware note and taped it to his office wall. “This,” he told new hires, “is why we stay vigilant.”

Chloe and Andre’s experiences were different—but they shared one lesson: **a hack doesn’t have to be the end.**

When it happens—and for many, it will—it’s what you do next that determines how much you lose, how fast you recover, and how strong you become.

You can panic... or you can act.

You can ignore it... or you can rebuild smarter.

You can beat yourself up... or you can become an example for others.

Because every victim who recovers, strengthens, and shares their story makes it harder for hackers to win the next time.

Chapter 9: Creating a Personal Security Plan

In a digital world where our lives, finances, businesses, and identities are deeply tied to the internet, **cybersecurity can no longer be reactive**—it must be proactive and routine. You can't rely on apps alone, or on your instinct to "spot something shady." Instead, you need a **system**—a personal cybersecurity plan that's clear, repeatable, and built into your weekly routine.

Think of it as your digital hygiene. Just as you brush your teeth and lock your doors, protecting your online life should be second nature. This chapter will guide you step-by-step through building a simple yet powerful personal cybersecurity system, regardless of your tech background.

Step 1: Perform a Security Audit of Your Digital Life

Start by identifying all the accounts, apps, and devices you use regularly. This includes:

- Email accounts (personal and work)
- Social media platforms
- Banking and payment platforms

- Cloud storage (Google Drive, Dropbox, iCloud)
- Online marketplaces (Amazon, Etsy, eBay)
- Mobile apps with personal data
- Work tools (Slack, Zoom, CRMs, client portals)
- Devices: smartphone, laptop, tablet, router, etc.

List them out. You can't protect what you haven't identified. This inventory becomes the foundation of your security plan.

Step 2: Organize and Strengthen Your Passwords

Use a password manager like **Bitwarden, 1Password, or Dashlane** to store and generate complex, unique passwords for every account.

- Replace any reused or weak passwords immediately.
- Create a system to check in every 3–6 months and update credentials for your most sensitive accounts.
- Avoid storing passwords in browsers or on sticky notes.
- Use **passphrases** (long combinations of random or meaningful words) when you need to remember one manually.

Remember: your email password is the most important one of all—it's the key to resetting everything else.

Step 3: Turn On Multi-Factor Authentication (MFA) Everywhere

If a service offers MFA, enable it. Prioritize:

- Email
- Banking and investing apps
- Cloud storage
- Social media
- Work logins
- Shopping platforms

Use **authentication apps** (like Google Authenticator or Authy) instead of SMS when possible. MFA significantly reduces the risk of account takeover—even if your password is compromised.

Step 4: Set Up Regular Data Backups

Create a backup routine for your important files, photos, documents, and device settings.

Recommended structure:

- **Daily or weekly backups** for critical work (use automation)
- **Local backup** on an encrypted external hard drive
- **Cloud backup** with services like iDrive, Backblaze, or Google One
- Test your backups quarterly to ensure they're recoverable

Label your backup drives clearly. Store at least one copy **offline** to protect against ransomware.

Step 5: Establish a Weekly Security Routine

Set aside 15–30 minutes weekly for personal cybersecurity. This "security hour" should include:

- Reviewing recent login activity on major accounts
- Checking for suspicious emails or messages
- Updating antivirus/anti-malware tools
- Running a quick system scan
- Reviewing and deleting unused apps

- Ensuring all devices are up to date with security patches

Set reminders in your calendar—consistency matters more than complexity.

Step 6: Secure Your Devices and Home Network

- **Enable auto-lock** on your devices and use PINs, biometrics, or strong passcodes
- **Turn off Bluetooth** and location services when not in use
- **Encrypt your devices** (this is standard on newer iOS and Android phones, as well as MacBooks)
- **Rename your Wi-Fi network** to avoid revealing device brands or your name
- **Use a strong Wi-Fi password** and change it every 6–12 months
- Log into your router settings and disable remote access and WPS
- Turn off "smart" devices you don't use or update them regularly

Step 7: Build Your Personal Incident Response Plan

If something goes wrong, have a playbook ready.

Create a simple checklist that includes:

- Steps to disconnect and isolate a device
- How to access password manager from a backup device
- Contact info for your bank, credit bureaus, and recovery services
- Instructions for wiping and restoring devices
- A list of accounts to reset immediately

Store this securely, both digitally and in a printed version.

Step 8: Educate Yourself and Your Inner Circle

Knowledge multiplies protection. Share what you learn with:

- Family members (especially kids, teens, and elderly relatives)
- Employees or team members
- Clients or customers (if you run a business)

Resources to explore:

- Free courses on cyber hygiene (Google, Cisco, or Coursera)
- Cybersecurity blogs (Krebs on Security, The Hacker News)
- Local workshops or webinars on digital safety

When the people around you are safer, **you're safer too**—because social engineering often uses your network against you.

Final Thoughts

Your personal cybersecurity plan should feel like a normal part of your life—not a burden. It doesn't require perfection, just intention. You don't have to outsmart every hacker on earth. You just need to make yourself a **harder target than the average person**.

Build the habit. Set the routine. Create your checklist. Share your knowledge.

In the final chapter, we'll discuss how to stay one step ahead in a world that's constantly evolving—and how to turn cybersecurity from a reaction into a mindset that protects you for life.

Ethan's personal cybersecurity plan

Ethan liked to think of himself as tech-savvy. He built websites for clients, kept his iPhone up to date, and even helped his parents set up their internet router. But after getting locked out of his bank account and watching over $3,000 in unauthorized transactions drain from his checking, he realized something important: **being tech-savvy doesn't mean being cyber-secure**.

It all started with a reused password. Ethan had used the same simple login—his favorite football team and birth year—for everything: PayPal, Gmail, Dropbox, his bank. When a small online retailer he'd once used got hacked, his credentials were leaked and published in a public database. A cybercriminal ran those credentials through a bot across hundreds of websites, and Ethan's accounts began to fall like dominoes.

He didn't know until it was too late.

After recovering his funds and going through weeks of email restoration and identity verification, he sat down one Saturday morning and did something most people never do: **he made a personal cybersecurity plan**.

He started by mapping out every online account he could remember—dozens of them, from Amazon to old subscriptions he hadn't used in years. Then he downloaded Bitwarden and began creating unique, randomly generated passwords for every account, syncing them securely to his devices.

Next, he enabled two-factor authentication on everything that allowed it. Even his social media and streaming services. He realized that a single breach of his email could unlock almost every other part of his life. So he made email the highest-priority asset—protected by MFA, monitored for unusual logins, and updated with a new password quarterly.

He didn't stop there.

Ethan bought a 1TB external hard drive and created backups of all client projects, financial documents, and photos. He stored one version offline and another in encrypted cloud storage. Then he turned off auto-connect on his devices so they wouldn't latch onto public Wi-Fi without his permission.

His laptop, once cluttered with browser extensions, was stripped down. He deleted unnecessary apps, removed access permissions from suspicious programs, and reviewed every setting he'd never bothered with before.

But what surprised Ethan most was how simple the process became once it was routine.

He blocked 30 minutes every Sunday for a "Security Check." It wasn't dramatic—he'd sip coffee while reviewing account activity, updating a few passwords, and scanning his system. Once a month, he'd refresh his backups and check for software updates. And once a quarter, he'd simulate a breach: testing his ability to restore files, access his password manager, and follow his own recovery plan.

It wasn't paranoia. It was preparation.

Ethan's story caught the attention of his clients. When one of them—a wedding photographer named Sara—had her online gallery wiped by ransomware, Ethan helped her recover. She hadn't backed anything up. The loss was devastating.

"That'll never happen again," she said through tears.

So Ethan helped her build her own security plan. And then another client. And another. Before long, he was teaching a monthly virtual workshop on "Cyber Self-Defense for Creatives." His plan had become a movement.

Elsewhere, a retired couple named Helen and Frank printed out their security checklist and taped it inside a kitchen cabinet. Every month, they checked off items together like a scavenger hunt—resetting passwords, scanning their devices, updating their router firmware. It became part of their rhythm. A shared ritual of digital safety.

And in a local high school, a 15-year-old named Jaya created a "Cyber Hygiene Club." She and her friends put together personal security kits for students: password manager guides, printed recovery checklists, backup tips, and safe browsing rules. They weren't experts. But they were **empowered**.

The common thread in all these stories? None of these people were cyber professionals. They were artists, retirees, freelancers, and students. What they shared was a commitment to **build simple systems before they were needed**.

Because no matter who you are or what you do, the digital world is your second home—and you should treat it like your first: locked, monitored, organized, and backed up.

Ethan now sleeps better. Not because he's invincible, but because he's prepared. And he knows that if something happens, he's no longer a passive victim. He's ready—with a plan.

Chapter 10: Staying One Step Ahead

Cybersecurity isn't a one-time action—it's an evolving process. Hackers adapt. Technology changes. New scams emerge. The moment you think you've "done enough," you risk falling behind. That's why the final and most important principle in your personal cybersecurity strategy is this: **stay one step ahead**.

The good news? Staying ahead doesn't require being perfect. It requires being **aware**, **updated**, and **willing to learn**. In this chapter, we'll break down long-term strategies to help you maintain and improve your defenses—without getting overwhelmed.

1. Stay Informed About Emerging Threats

Hackers move fast. Phishing tactics evolve. New malware variants are created daily. But by following reputable sources, you can stay current with minimal time investment.

Follow or subscribe to:

- *Krebs on Security* (krebsOnSecurity.com)
- *The Hacker News* (thehackernews.com)
- *Cybersecurity & Infrastructure Security Agency (CISA)*

bulletins

- *Have I Been Pwned* (haveibeenpwned.com) for data breach alerts
- *ThreatPost*, *Naked Security*, or *Dark Reading* for weekly digests

Even 10 minutes a week reading headlines will help you spot trends and react early.

2. Refresh Your Cybersecurity Habits Quarterly

Every 3 months, set aside time to:

- Update your most sensitive passwords (email, banking, cloud)
- Rotate recovery codes and MFA tokens
- Delete unused apps, accounts, or browser extensions
- Review your backup process and test a recovery
- Check permissions and privacy settings on apps and platforms

Cybersecurity isn't just about tools—it's about **maintaining behavior** over time.

3. Train Yourself to Think Like a Hacker

If you want to avoid getting hacked, learn how hackers think.

Ask yourself:

- “If I were trying to break into this system, what would I target?”
- “What data is most valuable to an attacker here?”
- “Which of my habits make me predictable or lazy online?”

This mindset makes you more skeptical, more alert, and less susceptible to manipulation. It also helps you catch weak spots in your own routines—before someone else does.

4. Upgrade and Evolve Your Tools Over Time

Just because an antivirus program or password manager worked two years ago doesn’t mean it’s the best choice today. As your needs grow, so should your tools.

Consider upgrading:

- From SMS-based MFA to app-based or hardware key MFA (like YubiKey)
- From free antivirus to a paid endpoint protection suite

if you run a business

- From basic cloud storage to encrypted backup platforms with version history

Reassess your tools once a year and replace anything outdated or unsupported.

5. Normalize Cybersecurity in Your Inner Circle

One of the best ways to stay ahead is to surround yourself with people who also take security seriously. That includes:

- Helping your family and friends build their own security routines
- Encouraging coworkers to verify suspicious emails
- Sharing resources when new scams are trending
- Creating a "security-first" culture if you run a business

When your network is informed, your risk decreases. Many breaches occur not from your device, but from someone you trust being compromised.

6. Use Alerts, Automation, and Monitoring Tools

You can't manually watch over every account or system, so let automation help.

Turn on these tools:

- **Login alerts** for email, banking, and cloud services
- **Dark web monitoring** offered by some password managers and credit bureaus
- **Automatic updates** for operating systems, antivirus, and apps
- **Security logs** and **access logs** on cloud drives or business dashboards

The more visibility you have into what's happening behind the scenes, the faster you can detect and respond to suspicious behavior.

7. Consider Insurance or Professional Support

If you run a small business, work with sensitive data, or simply want peace of mind, explore:

- **Cybersecurity insurance** that covers financial loss from attacks
- **Identity theft protection services** (like LifeLock or Aura)
- **Professional cybersecurity consultants** for audits

or setup

- **Legal guidance** on breach response, especially if you store client or customer data

Security isn't just a technical concern—it's a financial and legal one too.

8. Think Long-Term: Security as a Lifestyle

The people least likely to be hacked aren't those who install the fanciest software—they're the ones who make **small, consistent improvements** every week.

That includes:

- Delaying gratification when an urgent email arrives ("Let me verify this first.")
- Thinking twice before clicking links or downloading attachments
- Questioning convenience ("Is auto-login on a shared computer really safe?")
- Being okay with friction—like entering an MFA code—even when it's annoying

Just like staying healthy, cybersecurity is about **daily**

discipline, not panic-driven bursts of action.

Final Takeaway

Staying one step ahead doesn't mean knowing everything. It means refusing to stay still. Cybercriminals count on complacency. They hope you'll forget. Delay. Assume you're not a target.

But now you know better.

You've seen how they operate. You've learned the scams. You've built your system. You've tested your response.

And now, you're equipped to move through the digital world with **confidence**, **awareness**, and **control**.

In the final section of this book, we'll wrap everything up with a **summary checklist**, closing thoughts, and a reminder: security isn't just protection—it's empowerment.

How Maya got hacked

On a quiet Thursday morning, Maya Patel stood in her kitchen sipping coffee when her smartwatch buzzed. A notification from her Google account: **"New login detected from Taiwan."** She blinked. Taiwan?

She hadn't traveled in months. She tapped the notification,

opened her phone, and froze.

Her email had just been accessed by someone halfway across the world.

But instead of panicking, Maya moved calmly.

She opened her password manager, reset her Google login from a secure backup device, and revoked all app permissions. Then she enabled device verification, reviewed her recent logins, and logged the event in a personal security journal she'd created months earlier.

She wasn't shocked this had happened—only surprised it had taken this long.

Maya had been building her personal cybersecurity plan ever since a phishing scam stole her Airbnb earnings two years ago. Back then, she'd panicked, deleted important files, and spent weeks regaining access to accounts. But that experience had lit a fire in her. She vowed never to be caught off guard again.

She now approached cybersecurity like fitness—a habit, not a panic.

Every Sunday morning, she brewed coffee, put on music, and ran her **Security Sunday** routine:

- Reviewing recent logins and alerts

- Rotating key passwords
- Testing her offline backups
- Deleting unused accounts
- Reading the week's cybersecurity headlines

Her friends teased her for being overly cautious. "You act like a digital prepper," one of them joked.

But when her friend Alex got locked out of his Venmo after clicking on a fake customer support message on Twitter, it was Maya who helped him recover. She even showed him how to build his own security checklist, just like she had.

"Don't wait until it happens," she told him. "Plan like it already has."

Maya didn't have a cybersecurity degree. She wasn't in IT. She was a photographer with a business, a social media presence, and a personal archive of thousands of digital memories. She just treated those things with the same seriousness as a homeowner treats their locks.

And that made all the difference.

Elsewhere, in Boston, 62-year-old Victor and his wife Angela had built their own version of staying ahead. After falling for a fake Medicare call years ago, they took a class on cybersecurity at their local library. Now, once a month, they hosted a "Digital Safety Hour" with friends and neighbors.

They reviewed scam alerts, practiced phishing simulations, and helped each other set up MFA and password managers. What started as a reaction to a scare had turned into a neighborhood ritual.

"Most of our friends protect their physical homes," Victor said. "But they leave their digital front doors wide open."

Down in Austin, a small team of three women running an online coaching business set aside the first Friday of each month for what they called **"Cyber Sync."** It was part admin, part strategy, and part story-sharing.

They'd talk about new scam trends, update their platforms, share lessons from cyber incidents, and refresh their data protection policies.

When a hacker once tried to impersonate one of their client profiles to gain access to private course material, they caught it instantly. Not because of expensive software—but because they were **in the habit of checking**.

None of these people were experts. But they were alert. Intentional. Always improving.

They understood that cybersecurity wasn't about locking everything down and living in fear—it was about **maintaining awareness and adaptability** in a fast-moving digital world.

Maya's most important shift came not from installing a new app or reading a scary headline. It came from internalizing a mindset: **security is a lifestyle**.

It meant she no longer clicked links without hesitation. She no longer ignored update reminders. She no longer used public Wi-Fi to log into her bank or waited six months to update her passwords.

She didn't do these things because she was paranoid.

She did them because she respected her digital life—and knew that staying ahead meant **not falling behind**.

So when that hacker in Taiwan tried to gain access to her account, they didn't find a victim. They found a fortress.

And Maya? She simply finished her coffee, smiled, and opened her calendar.

"Security Sunday," she whispered. "Let's go."

From Target to Defender

The world we live in today is more connected than ever before. Every purchase, photo, login, and conversation passes through a digital gateway—an invisible infrastructure we rarely stop to examine. But as this book has shown, **what you don't see can hurt you**. Behind sleek interfaces and glowing screens are hidden threats—malicious software, phishing campaigns, impersonation schemes, and invisible eyes scanning for the next easy target.

And yet, with all this complexity, the core truth remains simple: **you have the power to protect yourself**.

We began this journey by pulling back the curtain on how hackers really work. We showed you their mindset, their motivation, and their tactics. We introduced you to tools like malware, ransomware, and keyloggers—not to scare you, but to arm you with knowledge. Because when you understand how something works, you stop being afraid of it—and start building strategies to counter it.

You saw real people make real mistakes. But you also saw them recover. You watched Chloe regain control of her digital business. You followed Maya as she turned caution into routine. You stood with Lisa, Derrick, Andre, and others as they confronted some of the worst-case scenarios—and emerged wiser on the other side.

Each story was meant to do more than inform. It was meant to reflect the reality we all share: **no one is immune. But everyone can prepare.**

The shift from being a digital victim to a digital defender doesn't require a degree, a title, or a certification. It requires **habit, curiosity, and a willingness to act before disaster strikes**.

It means choosing a unique password instead of the one you've always used.

It means pausing before you click that urgent email.

It means setting time aside every week to review what's protecting your digital life—and where the holes still are.

Most importantly, it means breaking the cycle of passivity.

For too long, cybersecurity has felt like someone else's job. Something handled by IT departments, tech support, or governments. But in a world where **everything is connected**, cybersecurity is now part of being an informed adult, a responsible business owner, a protective parent, and a trustworthy professional.

And it's never too late to start.

Maybe you're still catching up—using one password across multiple accounts. Maybe you've already been hacked. Maybe you've ignored those little red flags, hoping they'd go away on their own. That's okay.

Start today. Start now. Start small. But start.

Build your personal security plan. Share what you know with others. Turn awareness into action. Make it part of your identity to be proactive, not reactive. Not paranoid—**prepared**.

Hackers rely on assumptions. They assume you'll be lazy. Distracted. Untrained. Unprotected. But what they fear most isn't antivirus software or firewalls. It's **people who are paying attention**.

Let that be you.

Let this book be more than information. Let it be your new starting point. A foundation you can build on for years to come. As technology advances, so will threats. But so will your resilience—if you choose to grow with it.

So the next time you get a suspicious email, or someone asks you for personal information, or a website looks "a little off," you'll recognize it. You'll pause. You'll act with purpose. And you'll remember:

You're no longer the easiest target.

You're no longer someone who "didn't know better."

You're a defender now.

And that makes all the difference.

www.ingramcontent.com/pod-product-compliance
Lightning Source LLC
LaVergne TN
LVHW020234210926
848481LV00016B/2207
* 9 7 9 8 3 4 9 6 4 4 8 1 8 *